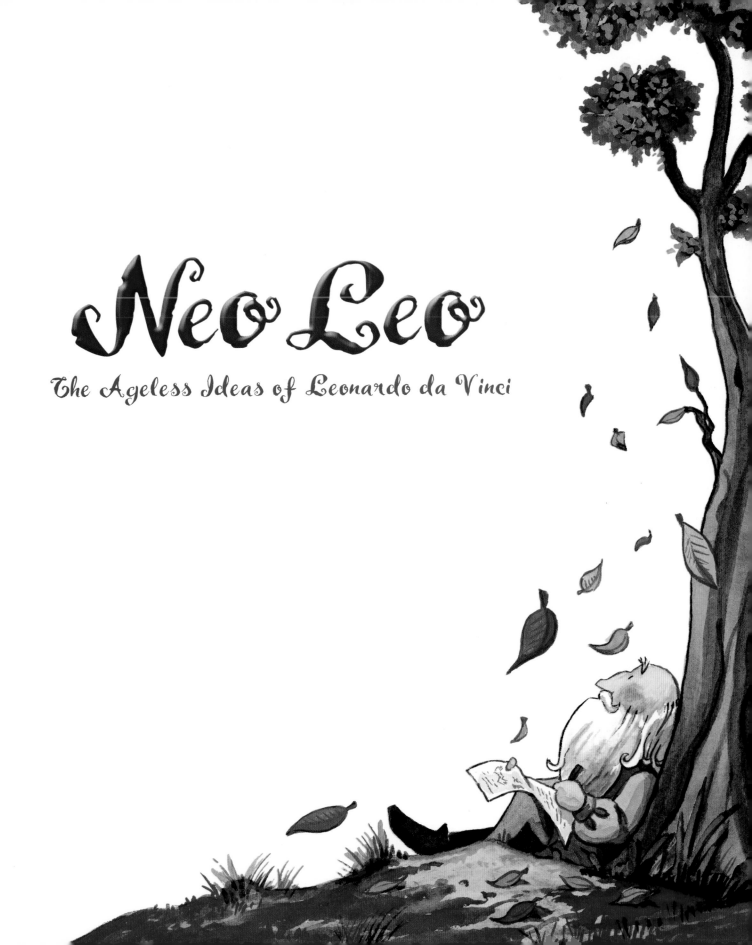

Neo Leo
The Ageless Ideas of Leonardo da Vinci

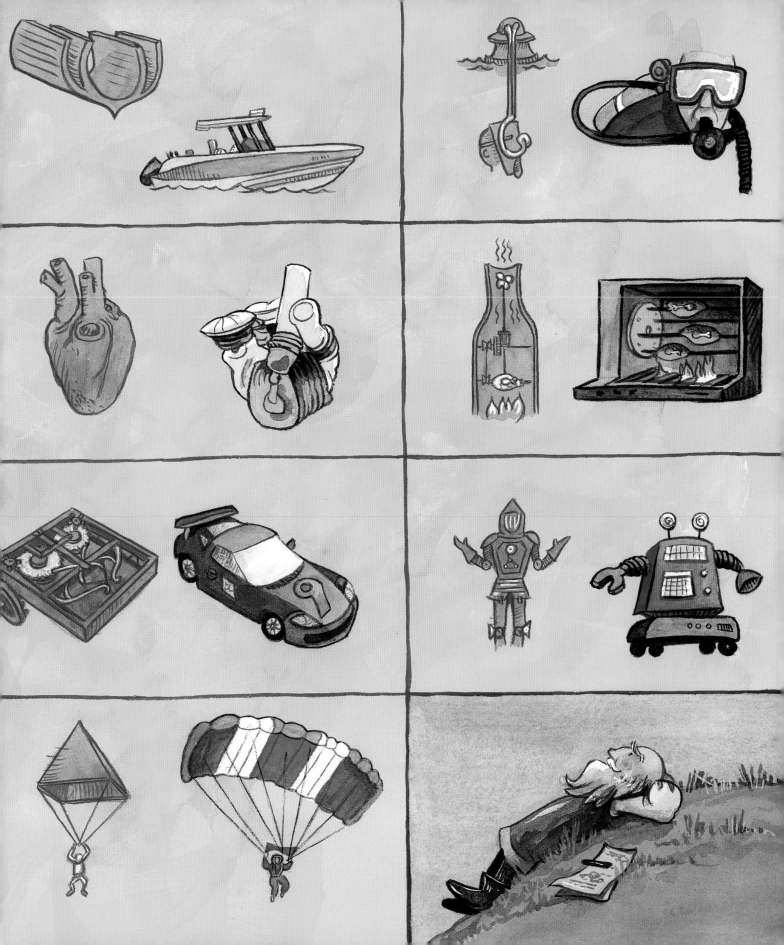

Author's Note

Reading Leonardo's original notes was a big challenge for historians.

After his death the notes were lost, sold, stolen, and scattered. So, it was quite a task to put the recovered pages back in order. Once that was accomplished, the challenge was not over. Leonardo always used mirror writing, which means that he wrote everything backward! To read the notes you have to hold them up to a mirror.

Here's an example:

ˈᎶɘɒɿninǫ ɘⱱɘɿ ɘxʜɒυƨƚƨ ƚʜɘ ɯinb. = Learning never exhausts the mind.

No one knows why he wrote backward. Some suggest that he wanted to make it difficult for people to read his ideas and steal them. Another theory is that writing backward prevented smudging his ink. Leonardo was left-handed and writing left to right across the page meant getting his left hand dirty in the fresh ink. Writing backward allowed him to write neatly, from right to left.

As you read through the book, try to decipher the mirror writing for extra information about Leonardo's inventions.

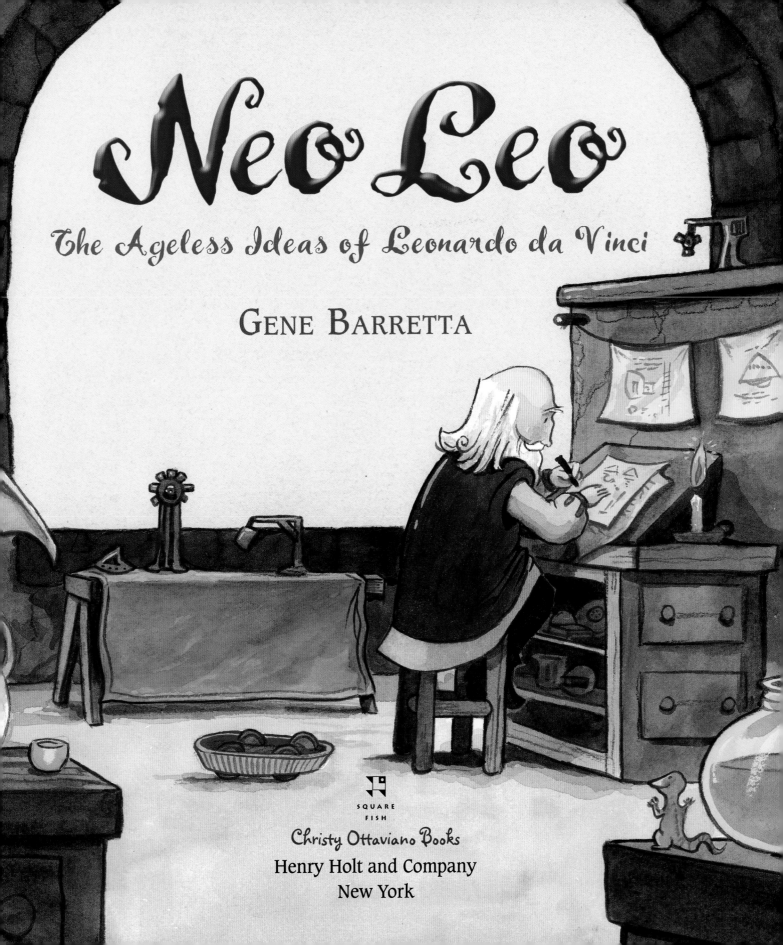

Neo Leo

The Ageless Ideas of Leonardo da Vinci

GENE BARRETTA

SQUARE FISH

Christy Ottaviano Books

Henry Holt and Company
New York

Leonardo da Vinci was fascinated by the world around him. He studied animals and people. He watched plants grow and birds fly. He explored the mighty rivers. Nature was his teacher. It inspired his remarkable studies and inventions.

Leonardo's ideas were revolutionary. But they remained buried among his 20,000 pages of notes. Most of his inventions were not built during his lifetime. The designs were either too expensive, too sophisticated, or too controversial.

Sadly, most of his ideas have been lost to time. But the surviving notes prove that he was a true visionary.

For example . . .

Neo

1903

The Wright Brothers are famous for creating an engine-powered aircraft that could carry a person into the sky.

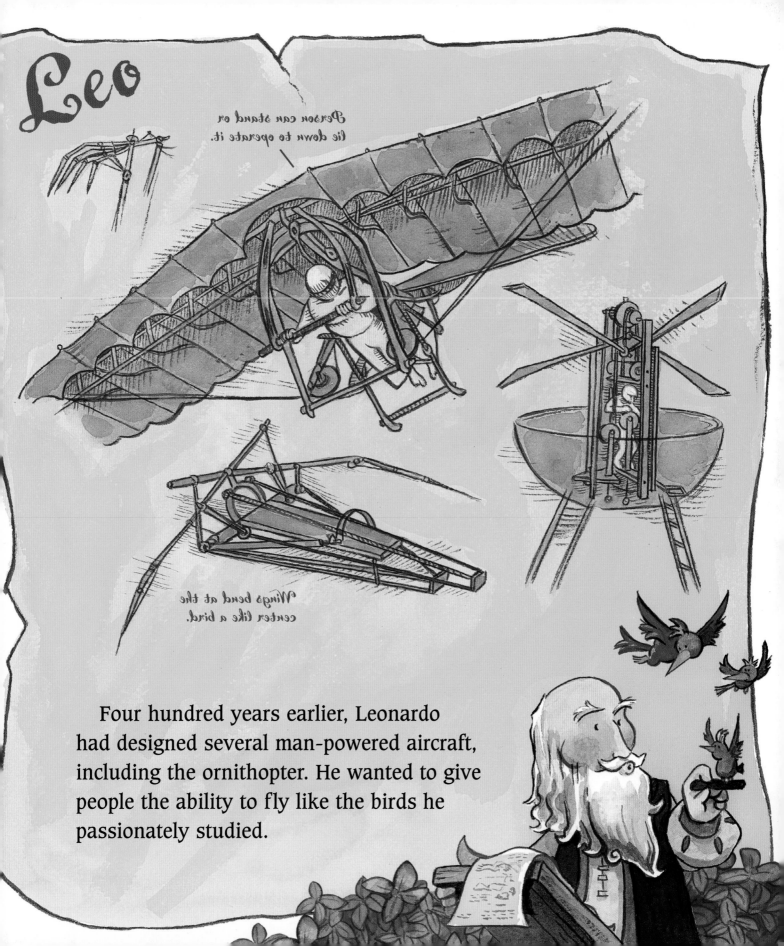

Four hundred years earlier, Leonardo had designed several man-powered aircraft, including the ornithopter. He wanted to give people the ability to fly like the birds he passionately studied.

Neo 1891

Otto Lilienthal had actually seen Leonardo's ornithopter drawings in the late 1880s.
He was motivated to develop history's first successful hang glider.

Leonardo designed his glider after
watching leaves glide through the air.

Neo

1887

Adolf Eugen Fick is responsible for making and fitting the first pair of successful contact lenses.

Oddly enough, he tested them on animals.

→

1895

Thomas Edison's Kinetoscope was the forerunner of the modern movie projector . . .

→

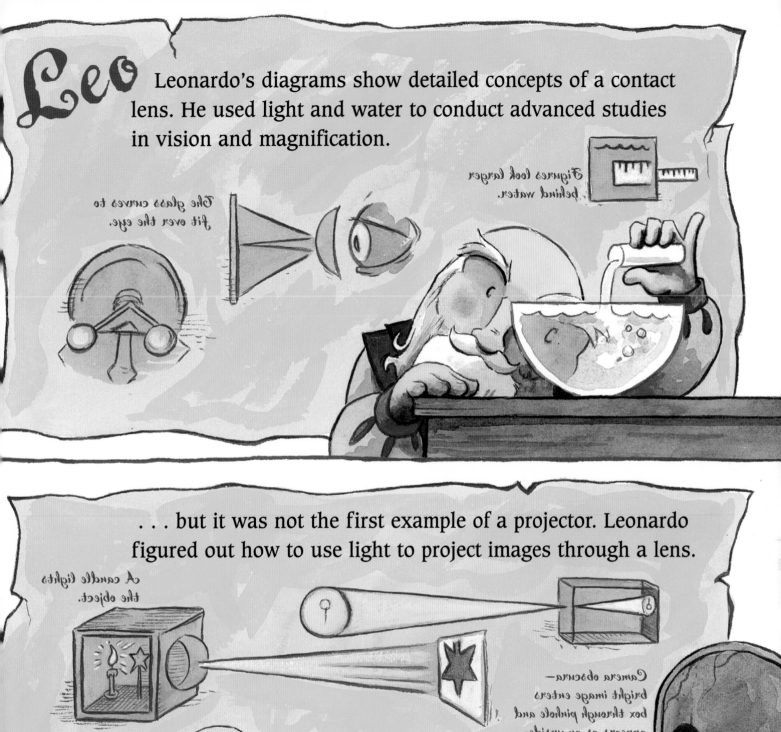

Leo Leonardo's diagrams show detailed concepts of a contact lens. He used light and water to conduct advanced studies in vision and magnification.

The glass curves to fit over the eye.

Figures look larger behind water.

. . . but it was not the first example of a projector. Leonardo figured out how to use light to project images through a lens.

A candle lights the object.

The convex glass magnifies the image.

Camera obscura— bright image enters box through pinhole and appears as an upside-down picture inside the box.

Neo 1781

Thomas Paine exhibited a model of his single-span bridge in Benjamin Franklin's garden. At the time, no one believed his bridge could work, especially without the usual support piers to hold up the center.

Leo

Leonardo believed that a single-span bridge was surely possible. But like Mr. Paine, he never saw his bridge constructed. He also proved the value of truss bridges. Leonardo's experiments confirmed that a triangular truss would resist tension better than the older box structures. He proposed a two-level truss bridge—the bottom level for transportation and the top level for pedestrians.

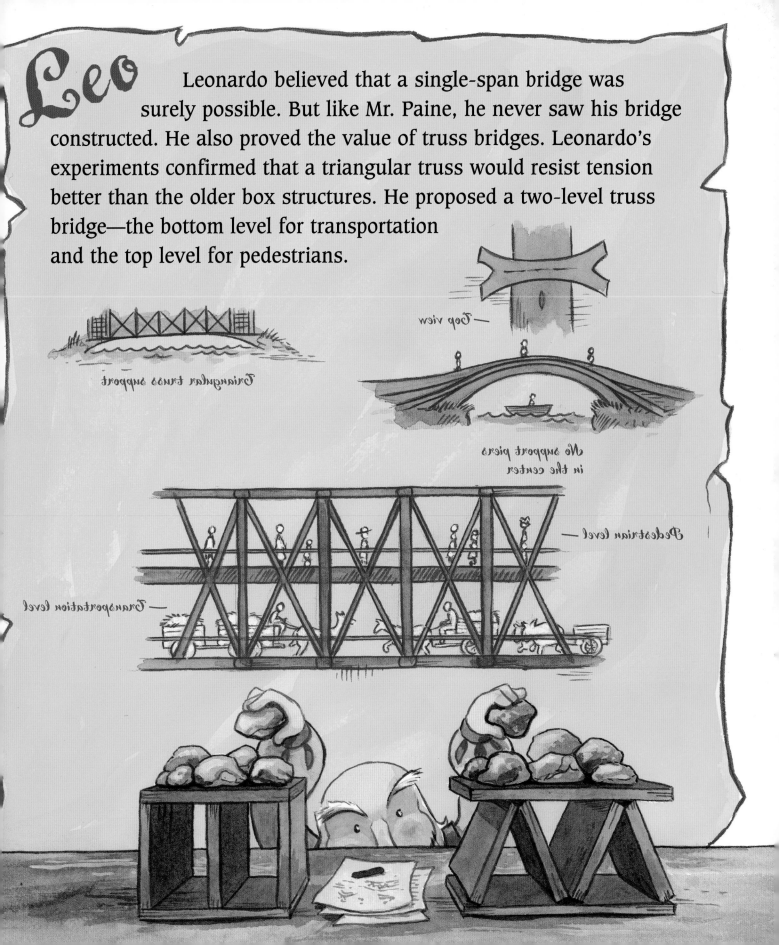

Top view

Triangular truss support

No support piers in the center

Pedestrian level

Transportation level

Neo

1916

The world had not seen a tank in action until World War I. The British Navy developed it, and Captain H. W. Mortimore brought one into battle for the first time.

Leo

Open-air top

Four men operate the cranks.

Guns around entire tank

Wheels turn on a crank.

Leonardo was thinking about tanks long before Captain Mortimore. Turtles became his model. He considered himself a pacifist but looked at weapons as a design challenge. He also designed grenades, machine guns, and a giant catapult, among others.

Neo 1870

James Starley is credited as the father of the British bicycle industry. Many of his inventions led us closer to the type of bicycles we ride today.

Leo

Gears with squared teeth do not work. Later, he rounded them to make the chain function.

A design for a chain link

Drawing is too amateurish for Leonardo

Did Leonardo invent the bicycle?

A bicycle does appear in Leonardo's notes. While historians agree that it is not his drawing, some think that a pupil drew it after studying a bicycle prototype in Leonardo's workshop. Others say it was drawn as a prank by someone centuries later.

We may never know for sure, although we do know that Leonardo had designed many parts that are used to build bicycles, such as gears and chains.

Neo

1907

Paul Cornu was a bicycle maker by trade. He built the very first helicopter to lift off vertically. It hovered one foot above the ground for twenty seconds.

Leo

Four men operate it.

Wings turn
like a screw.

Air compressed
under wing.

Prior to that, Leonardo devised his own version
of the helicopter—the helical screw. It used the same
principle as modern helicopters for compressing air
to achieve liftoff.

Unfortunately, the weight of his machine and
the man-powered mechanics would have prevented
real flight.

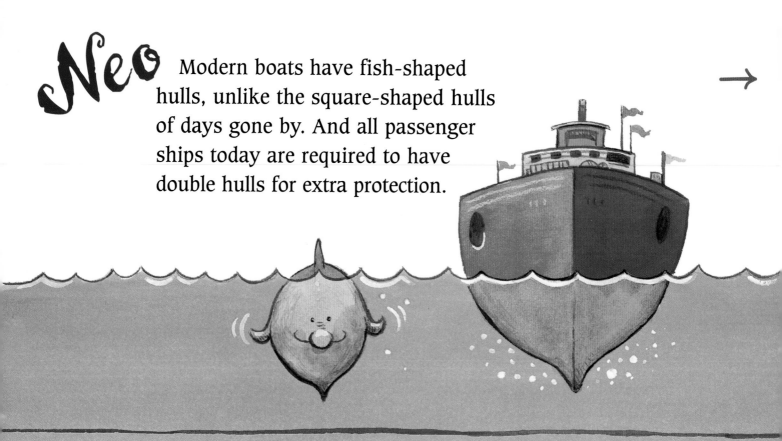

Neo Modern boats have fish-shaped hulls, unlike the square-shaped hulls of days gone by. And all passenger ships today are required to have double hulls for extra protection.

→

1943

Jacques Cousteau and Emile Gagnan made modern diving equipment popular when they designed underwater breathing equipment called the Aqua-Lung.

→

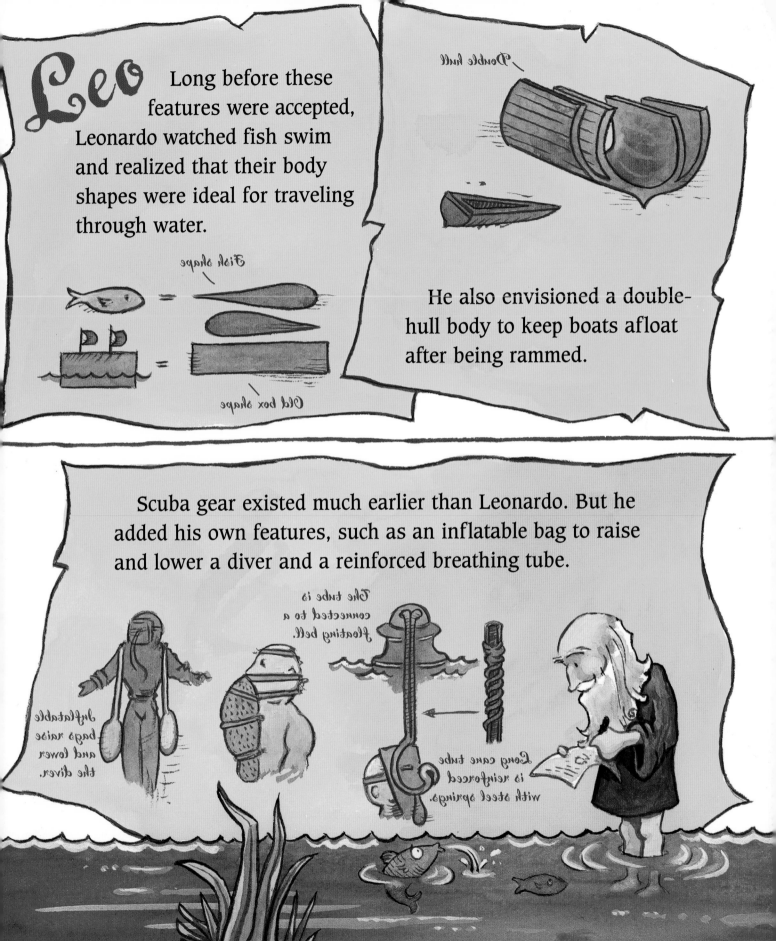

Leo Long before these features were accepted, Leonardo watched fish swim and realized that their body shapes were ideal for traveling through water.

Fish shape

Old box shape

Double hull

He also envisioned a double-hull body to keep boats afloat after being rammed.

Scuba gear existed much earlier than Leonardo. But he added his own features, such as an inflatable bag to raise and lower a diver and a reinforced breathing tube.

The tube is connected to a floating bell.

Inflatable bags raise and lower the diver.

Song cane tube is reinforced with steel springs.

Neo With the use of modern imaging technology, doctors now understand that when blood moves through the heart, it forms a vortex that opens and closes the valves.

Leo

Leonardo had already figured it out. Through detailed body dissection and simulated water experiments, he discovered and diagrammed accurate examples of vortex formation in the blood.

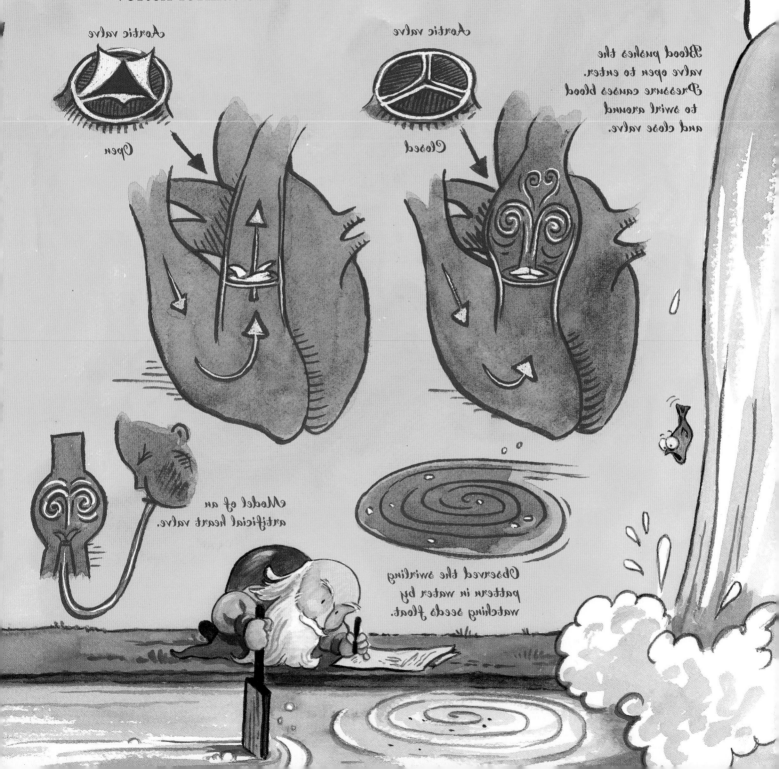

Neo What do a steam locomotive and a cooking rotisserie have in common? Leonardo da Vinci, of course.

Leo

His notebooks are filled with experiments on steam power and air pressure, predicting the development of the steam engine. He understood that hot air rises and used that knowledge to operate an automatic rotisserie. The first!

Steam expands and forces the lid to rise.

Heated water makes steam.

Hot air rises and turns a fan.

The fan turns the rotisserie.

Neo

1885

Automobile engineer Karl Benz invented the first gas-powered automobile and essentially launched the auto industry.

1940

When people attended the 1940 World's Fair in New York they came face-to-face with Elektro and Sparko, two of the world's earliest robots.

Leo

Leonardo's self-propelled cart foreshadowed both the automobile and the robot. The cart was spring-powered. Levers and gears were used to program its movements like a primitive robot.

Leonardo designed and actually constructed robots for royalty and court pageants. Springs, levers, water, and weights powered and controlled them.

Steering system

Could sit and stand

Coil springs beneath toothed gear heads

Pedals controlled steering system.

Regulated the timing of springs

Wheels underneath

Lion's chest opened and flowers spilled out.

Steering device

Neo **1785**

Jean-Pierre Blanchard created the original all-fabric parachute and was the first to prove that it could provide safe escape from a hot-air balloon. Actually, his dog proved it.

Leo

Or one could argue that Leonardo proved it before both of them. He had a different purpose for his parachute. Its function was for traveling from high to low surfaces like the birds he observed. His triangle design, unfortunately, was never tested . . .

Closely woven linen

24 feet squared
by 24 feet high

Air pressure helps
the parachute float.

. . . until now!

That's right. Leonardo's ideas are finally coming to life. Several are being built and tested. And they are working!

Adrian Nicholas built and flew Leonardo's parachute.

Vebjørn Sand's team built the single-span bridge.

Mark Rosheim built and operated the self-propelled cart and robot knight.

Dr. Mory Gharib built and confirmed the success of Leonardo's artificial heart valve model.

Steve Roberts and Martin Kimm built Leonardo's glider. Judy Leden flew it.

The amount of knowledge and vision found in Leonardo's notes is overwhelming. And remember—about two-thirds of his notes are still missing! Imagine what is left to learn from this incredible inventor.

Bibliography

BOOKS

Cooper, Margaret. *The Inventions of Leonardo da Vinci*. New York: Macmillan, 1965.

Laurenza, Domenico. *Leonardo's Machines: Da Vinci's Inventions Revealed*. Edited by Mario Taddei and Edoardo Zanon. Cincinnati: A David & Charles Book, 2006.

Reti, Ladislao, ed. *The Unknown Leonardo*. New York: McGraw Hill, 1974.

WEB SITES

The Leonardo Museum in Vinci. www.museoleonardo.it/eng.

National Museum of Science and Technology: Leonardo Da Vinci. www.museoscienza.org/english.

Universal Leonardo. www.universalleonardo.org.

DVDS

Leonardo's Dream Machines. PBS Home Video, 2005.

The Life of Leonardo da Vinci: The Most Brilliant Mind in History. Chicago: 2003.

Modern Marvels: Da Vinci Tech. The History Channel, 2005.

To Nella and Bruce Storm,
for making the Renaissance
come alive for a ten-year-old.
Most boys wanted to be astronauts
or firemen; I wanted to be Leonardo.

Love, your dear boy
—G. B.

SQUARE
FISH

An Imprint of Macmillan
120 Broadway,
New York, NY 10271
mackids.com

NEO LEO. Copyright © 2009 by Gene Barretta.
All rights reserved. Printed in China by RR Donnelley Asia Printing Solutions Ltd.,
Dongguan City, Guangdong Province.

Square Fish and the Square Fish logo are trademarks of Macmillan and
are used by Henry Holt and Company, LLC under license from Macmillan.

Our books may be purchased in bulk for promotional, educational, or business use.
Please contact your local bookseller or the Macmillan Corporate and Premium Sales Department
at (800) 221-7945 ext. 5442 or by e-mail at MacmillanSpecialMarkets@macmillan.com.

Library of Congress Cataloging-in-Publication Data
Barretta, Gene.
Neo Leo : the ageless ideas of Leonardo da Vinci / Gene Barretta.
p. cm.
Includes bibliographical references.
ISBN 978-1-250-07960-2 (paperback)
1. Inventors—Italy—Biography—Juvenile literature. 2. Leonardo, da Vinci, 1452–1519—
Knowledge—Engineering—Juvenile literature. 3. Inventions—History. I. Title.
T40.L46B37 2009 609.2—dc22 2008038220

Watercolor on Arches cold-press paper was used to create the illustrations for this book.

Originally published in the United States by Christy Ottaviano Books/Henry Holt and Company, LLC
First Square Fish Edition: 2016
Book designed by April Ward / Square Fish logo designed by Filomena Tuosto

7 9 10 8

AR: 0.5 / LEXILE: AD930L